Portraits and Souls

Book 1

Portraits remind us of other people.

Photos and words by Roditch.

Copyright

Copyright©Roditch
All rights reserved.

Dedicated to Reuben Hedditch, an awesome musician.

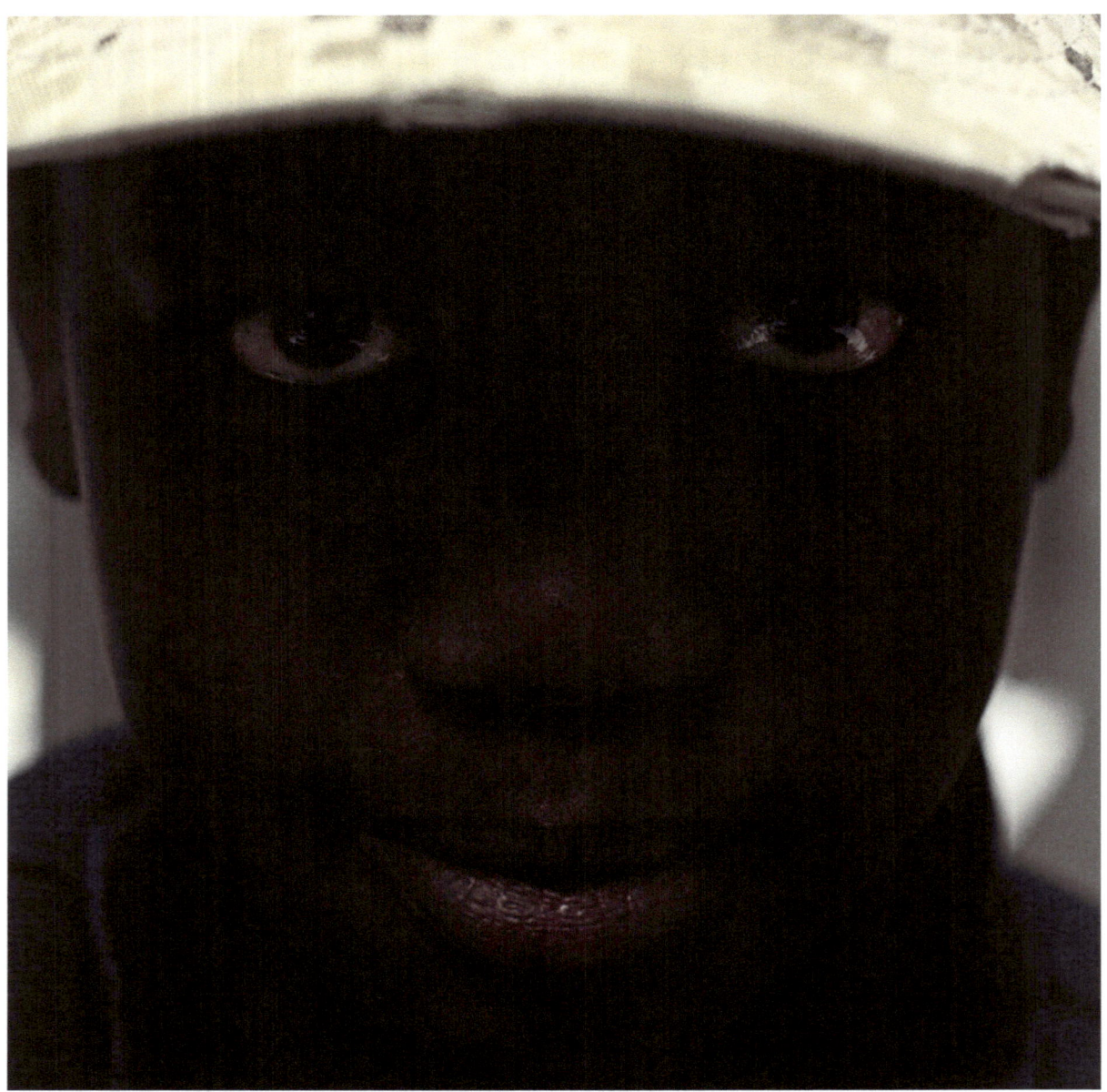

My family are ghosts
behind their fate

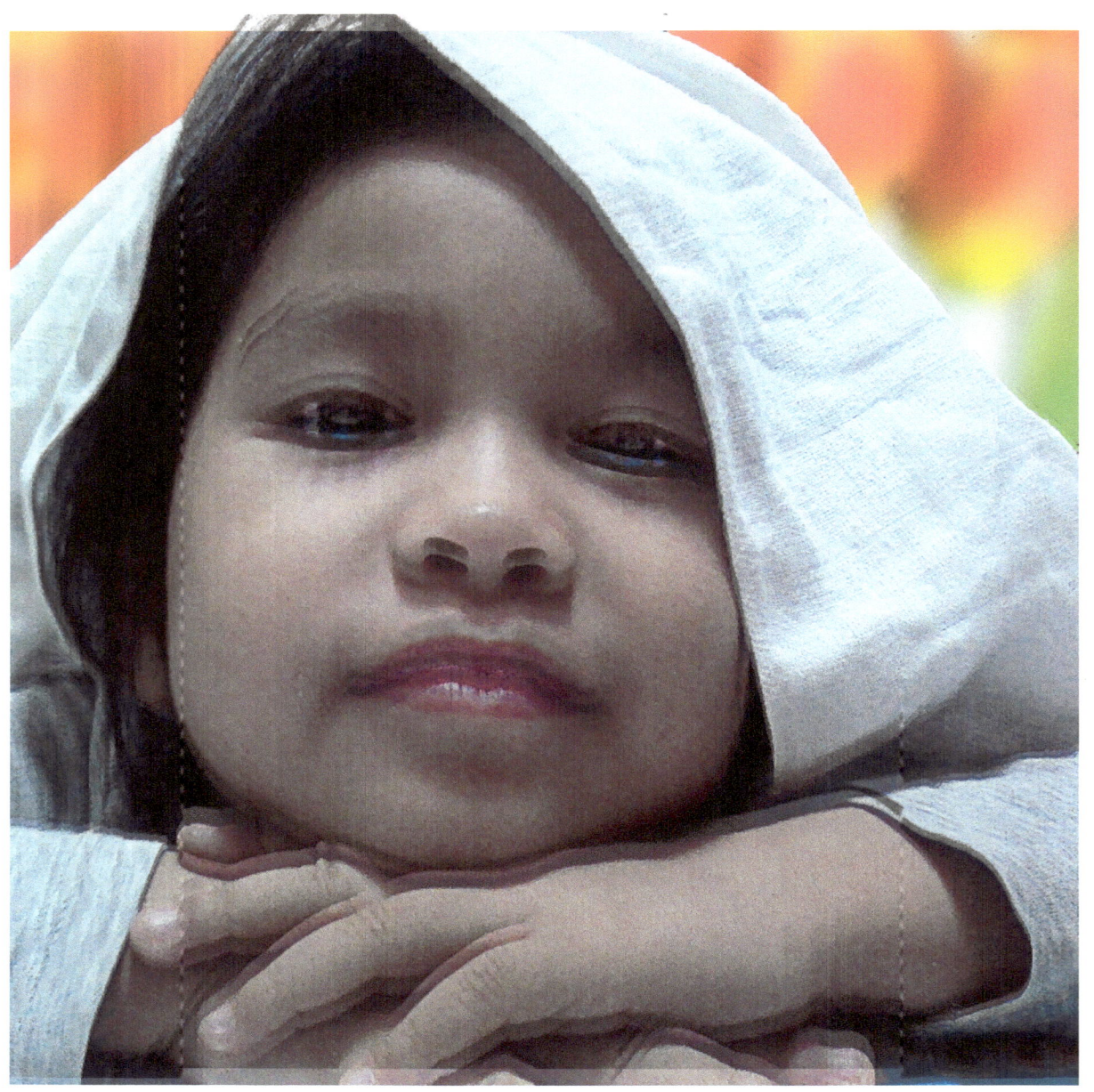

Let's be fiends and chatter our chatter

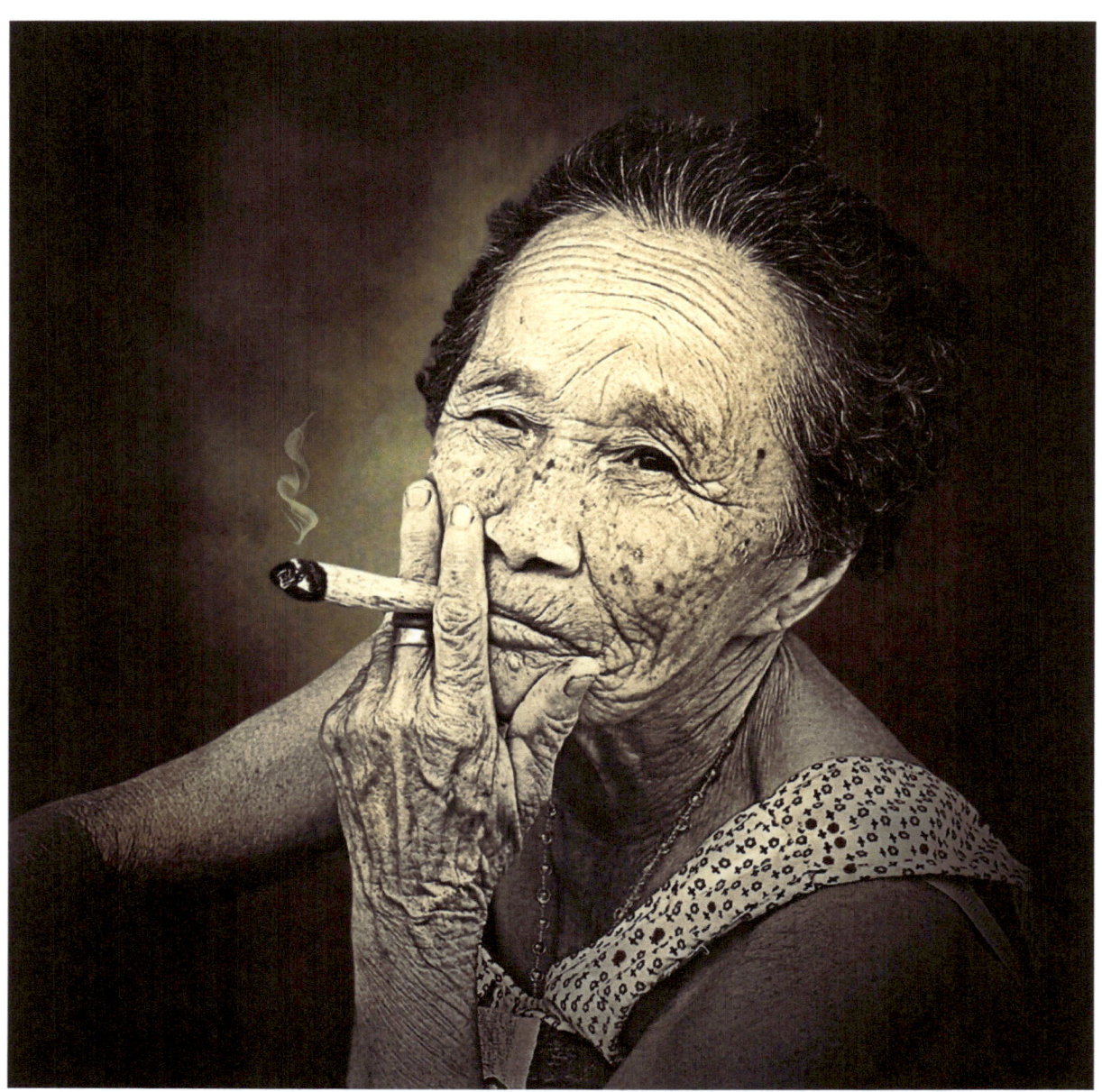

No one is still not listening.

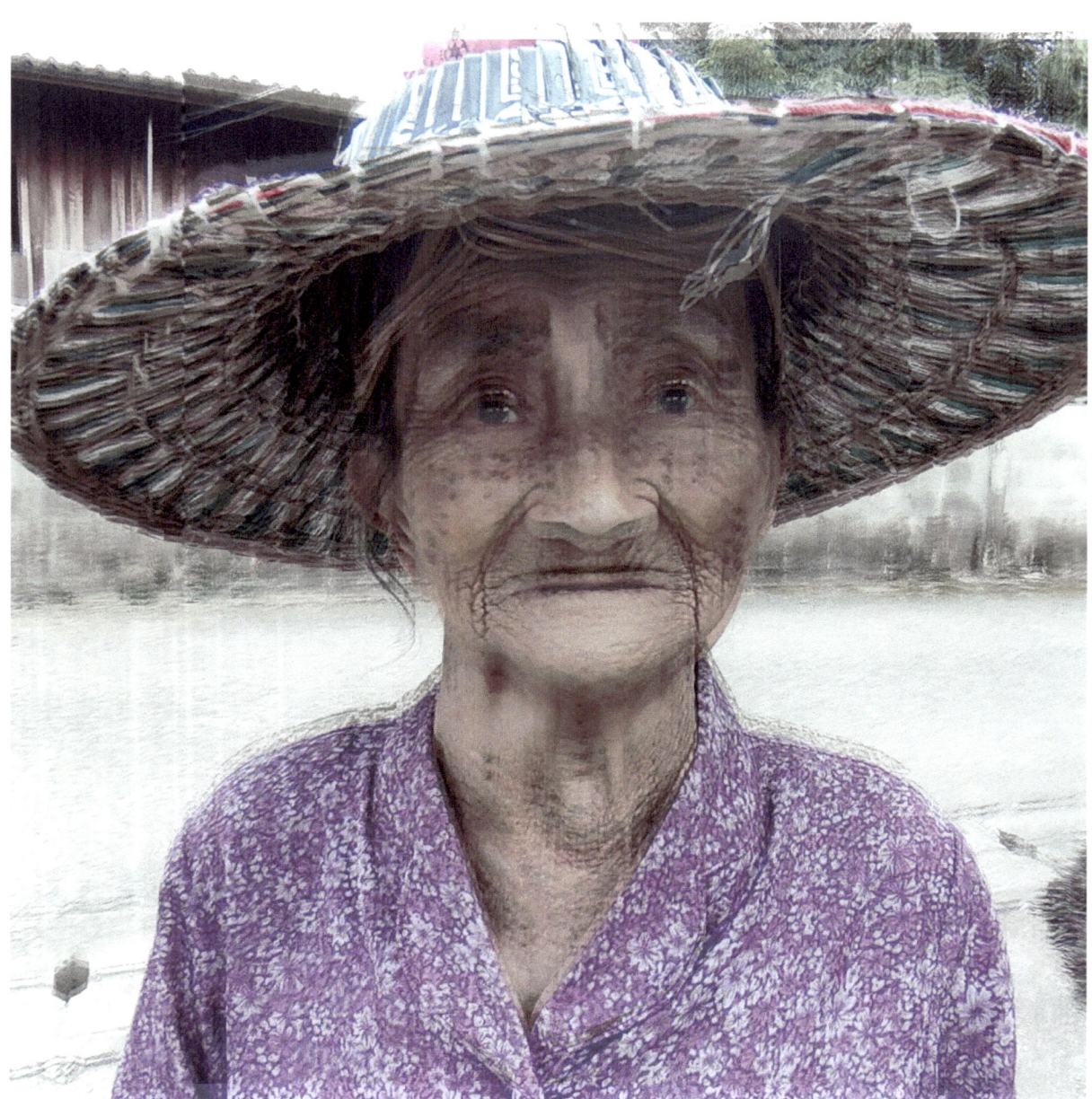

One will to humble

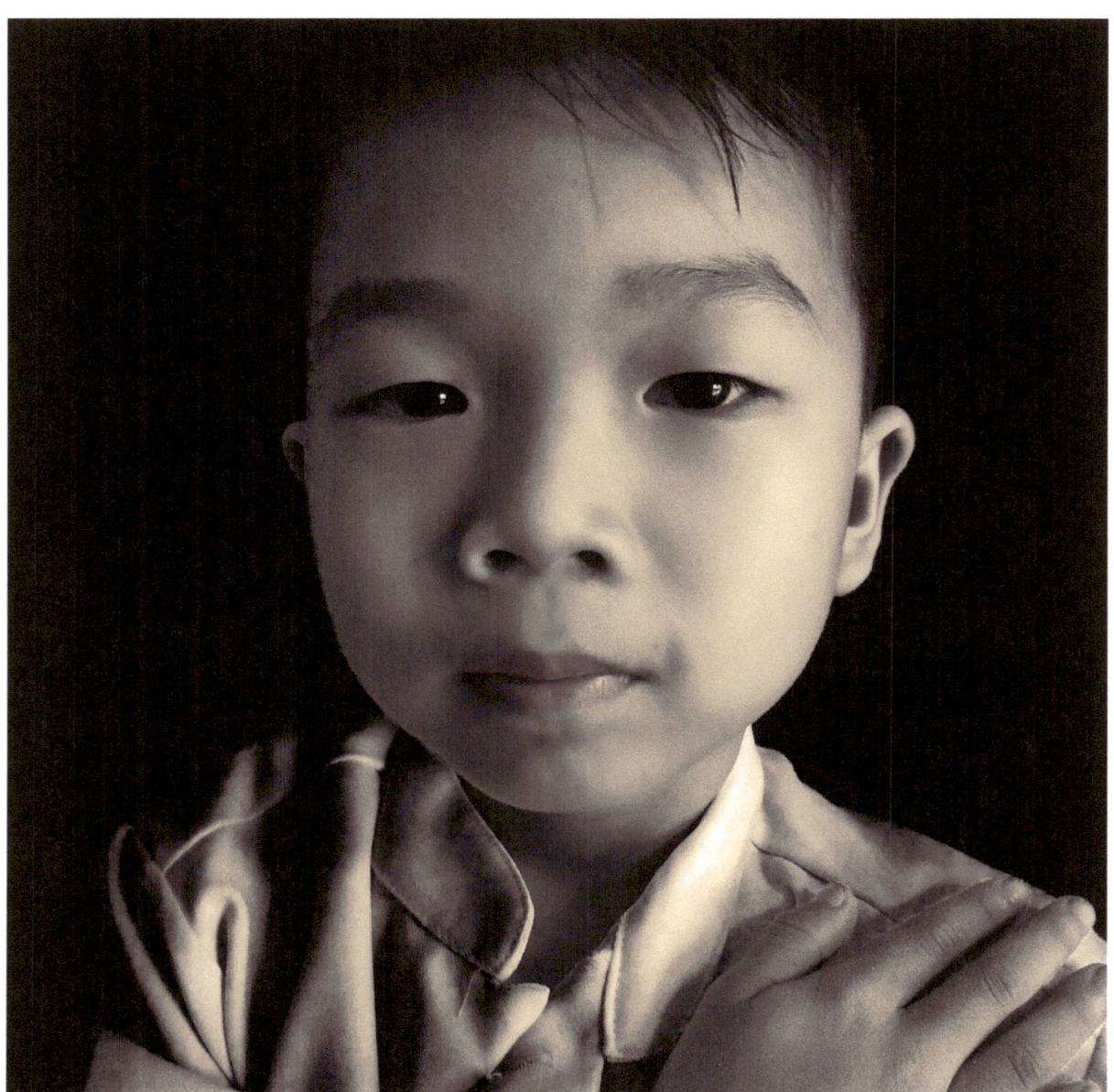

How do we grow our children,
spades, hearts, clubs
or diamonds?

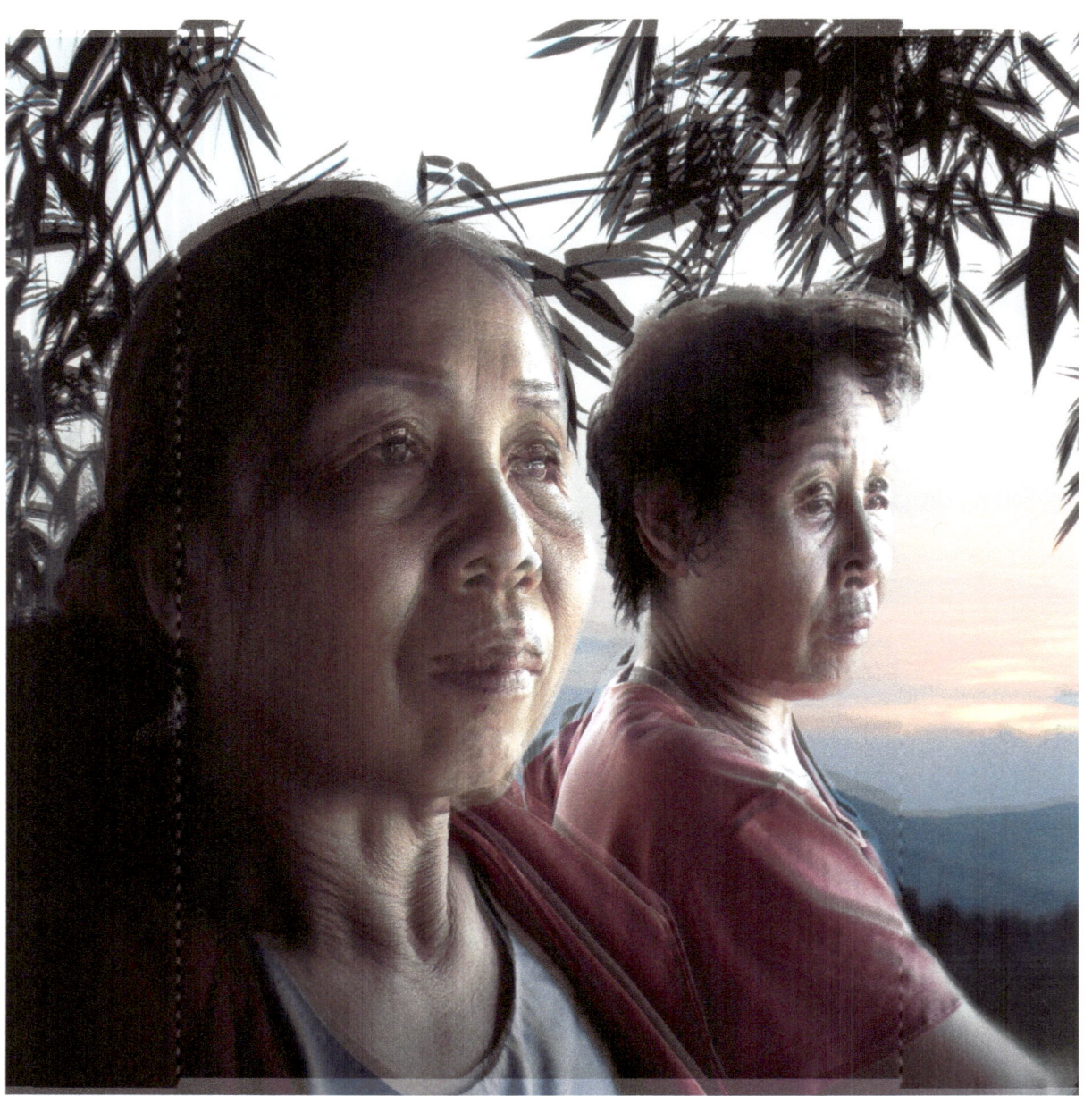

Make it lighter

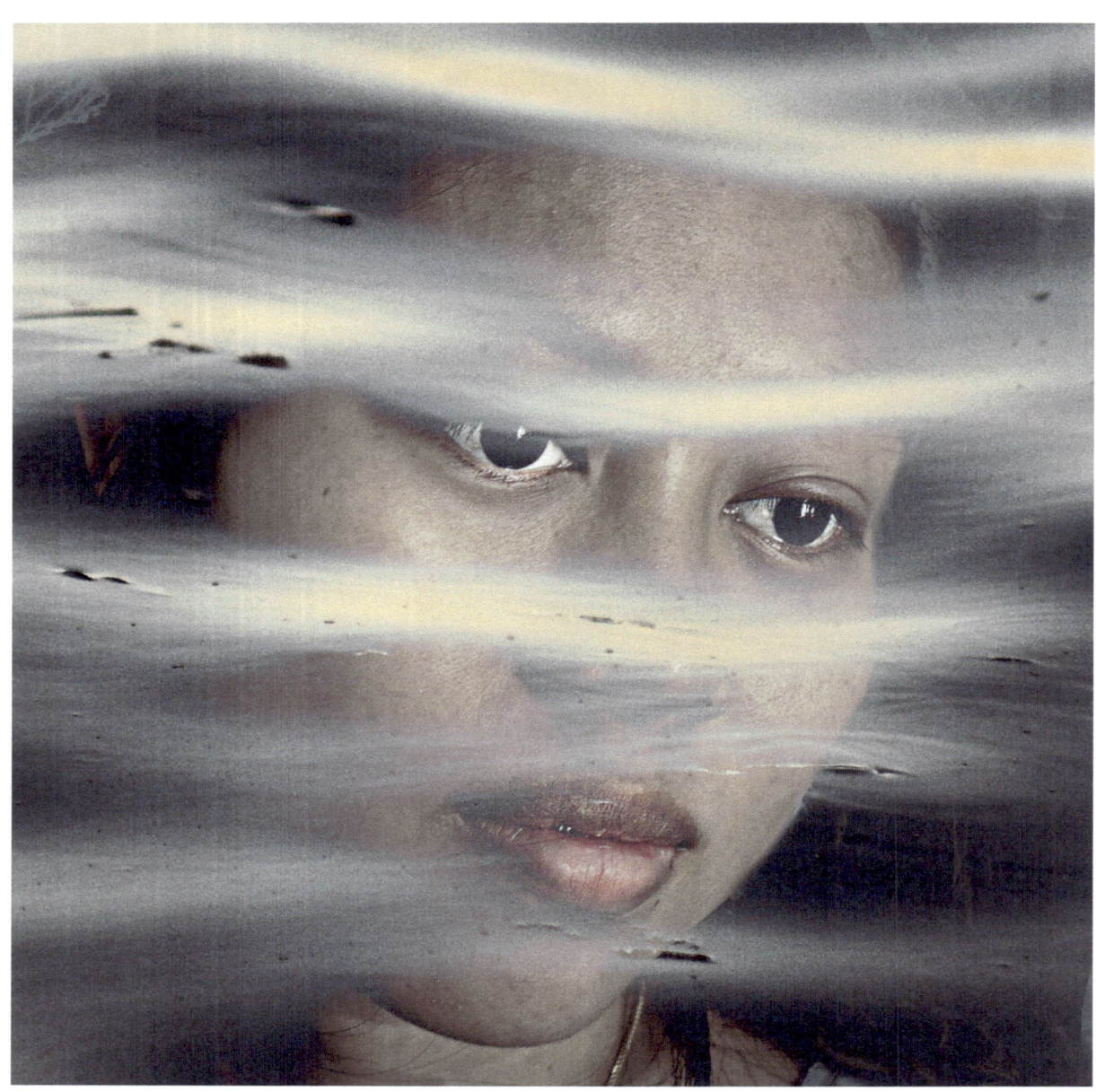

Wat makes me happy

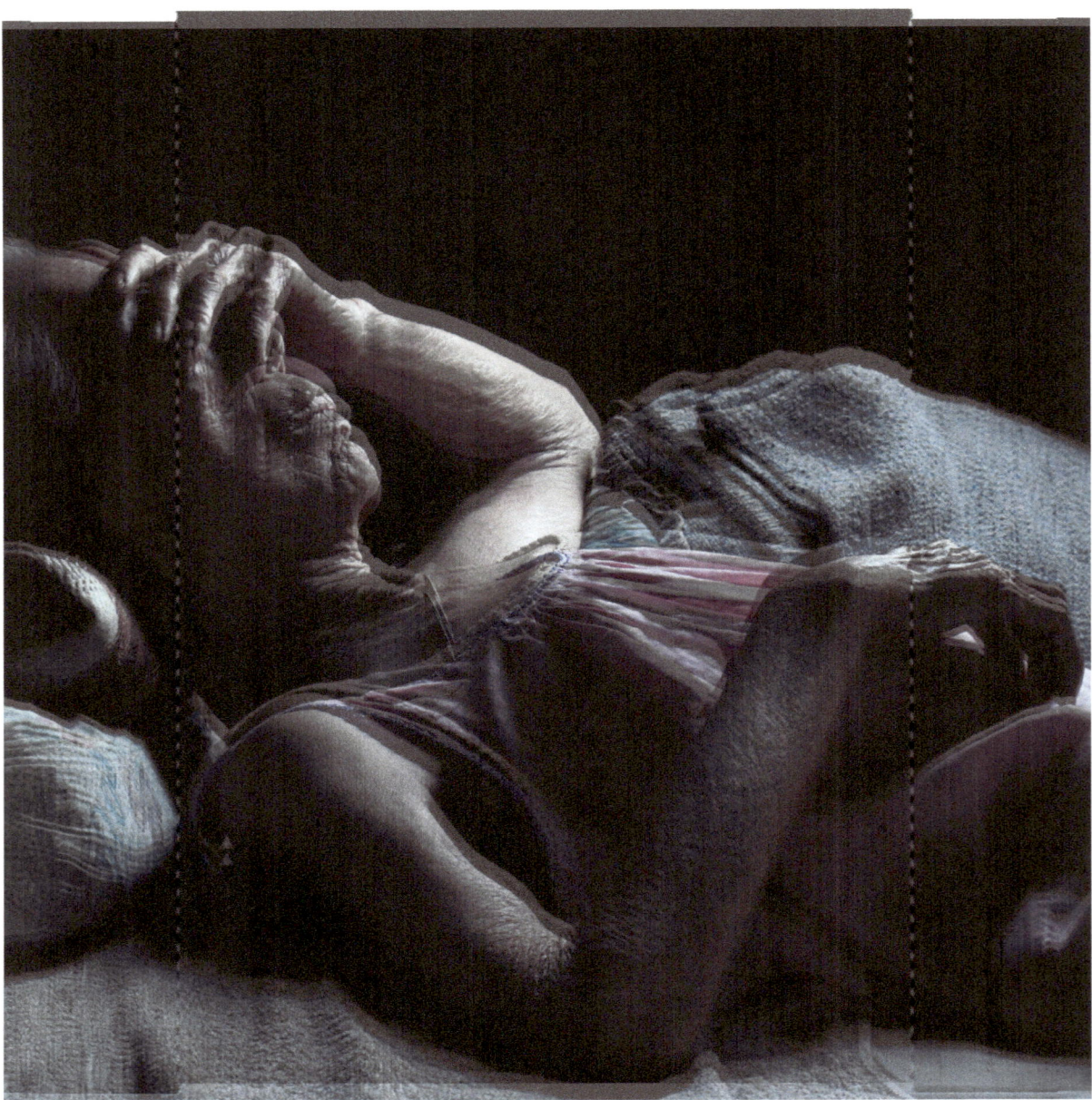

Alcohol kills the pain, not the problem

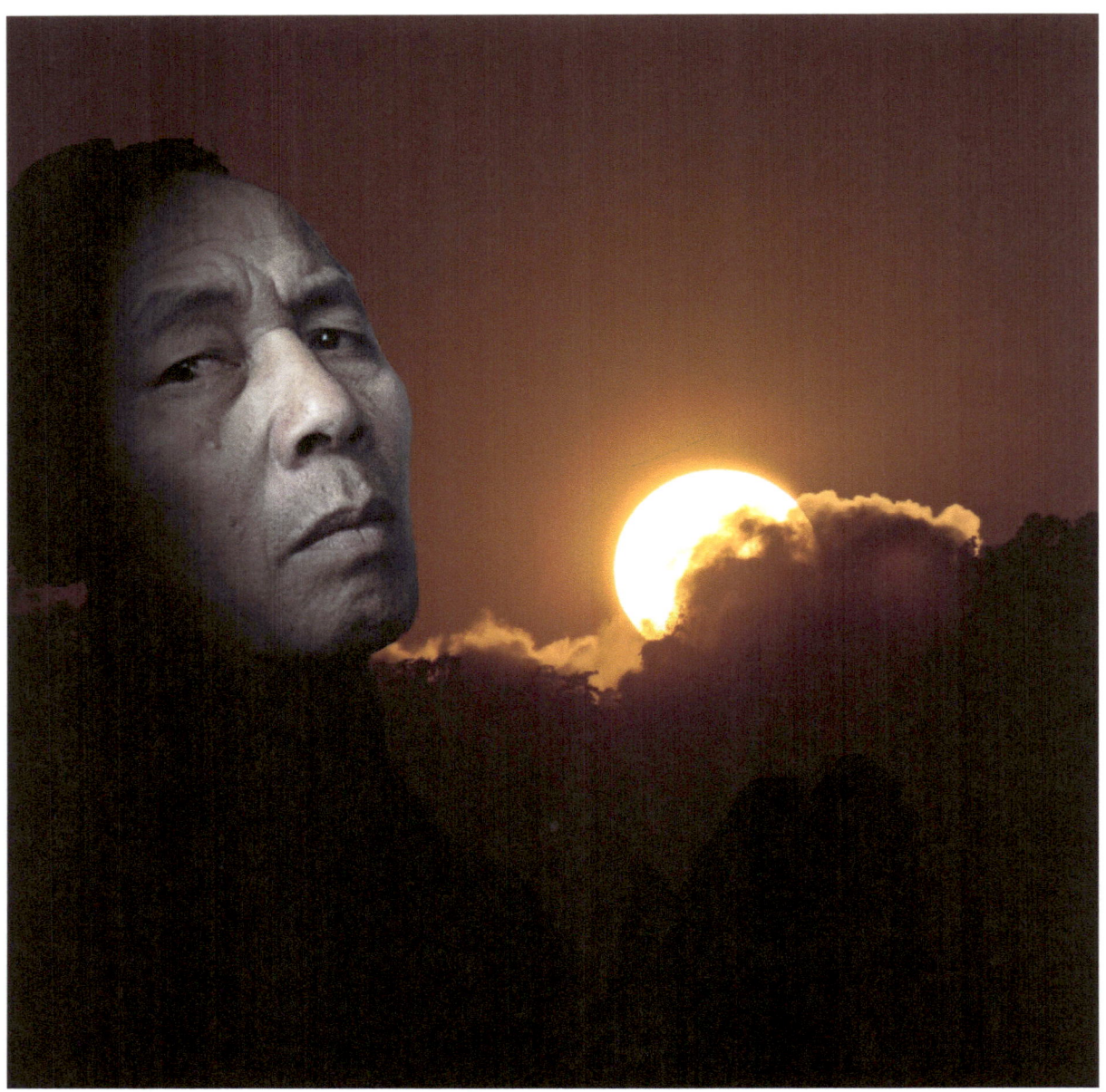

Grand Turino is
no bullshit

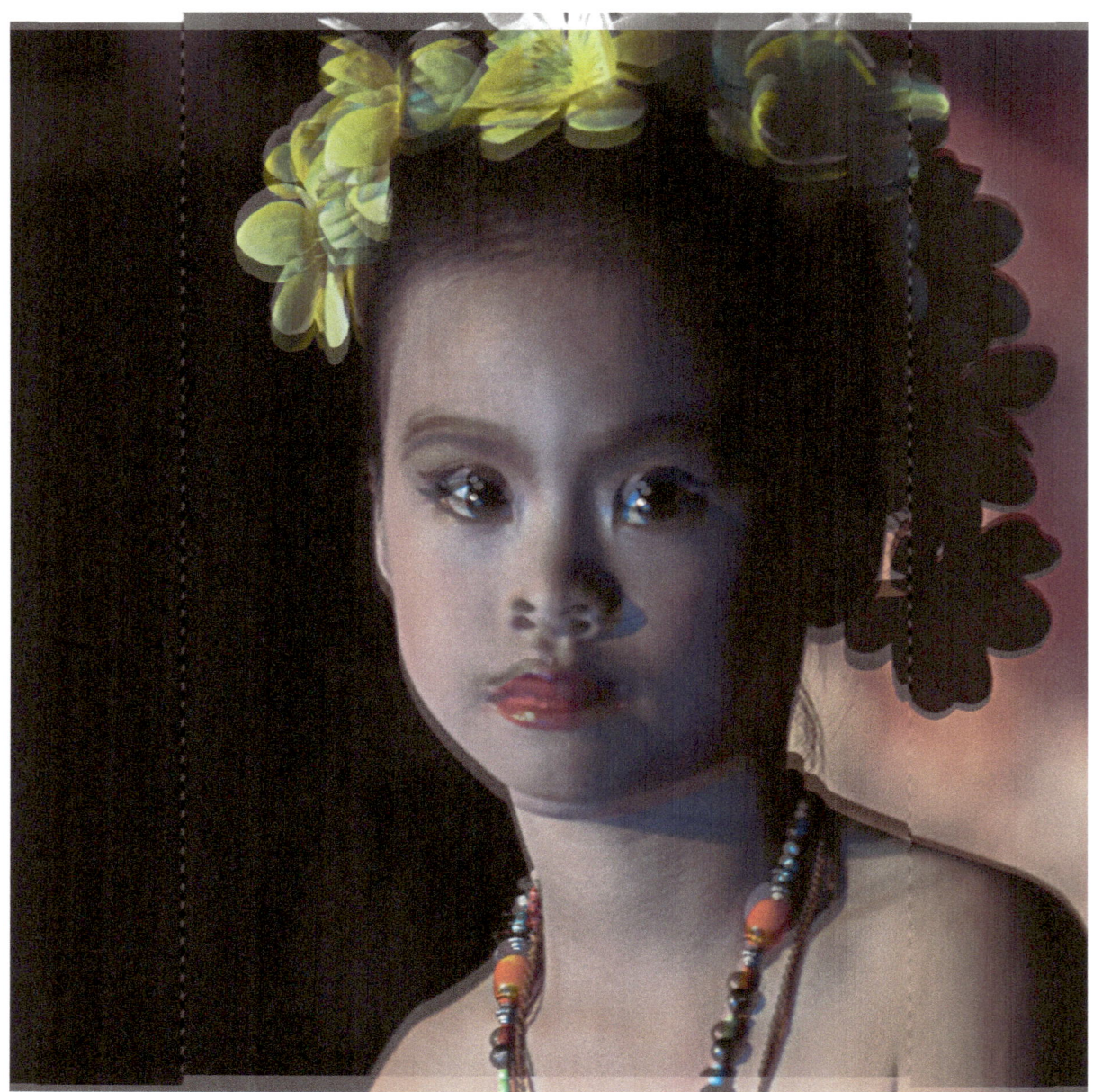

Love, and the give and take deals

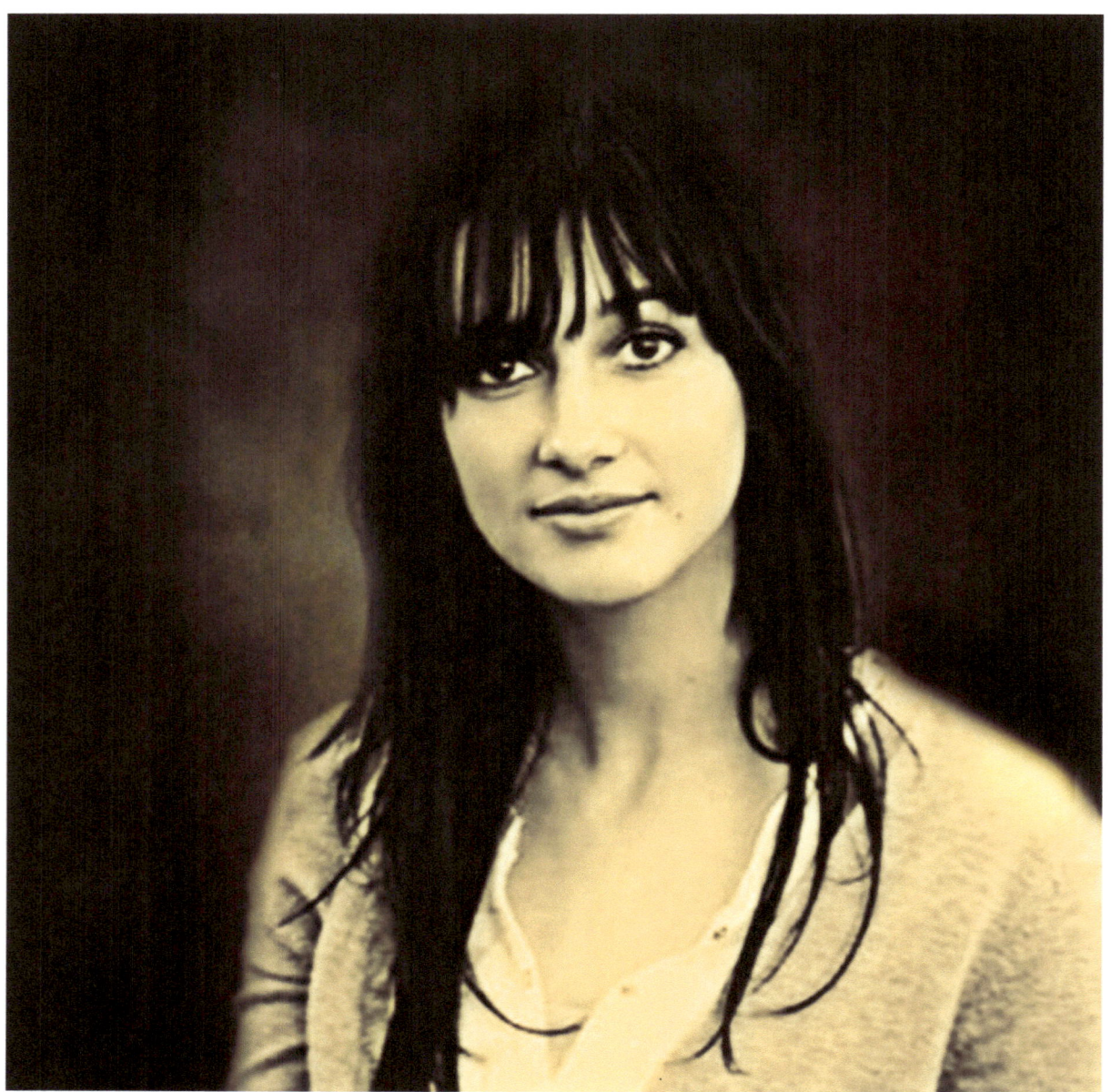

Art is science
from the soul

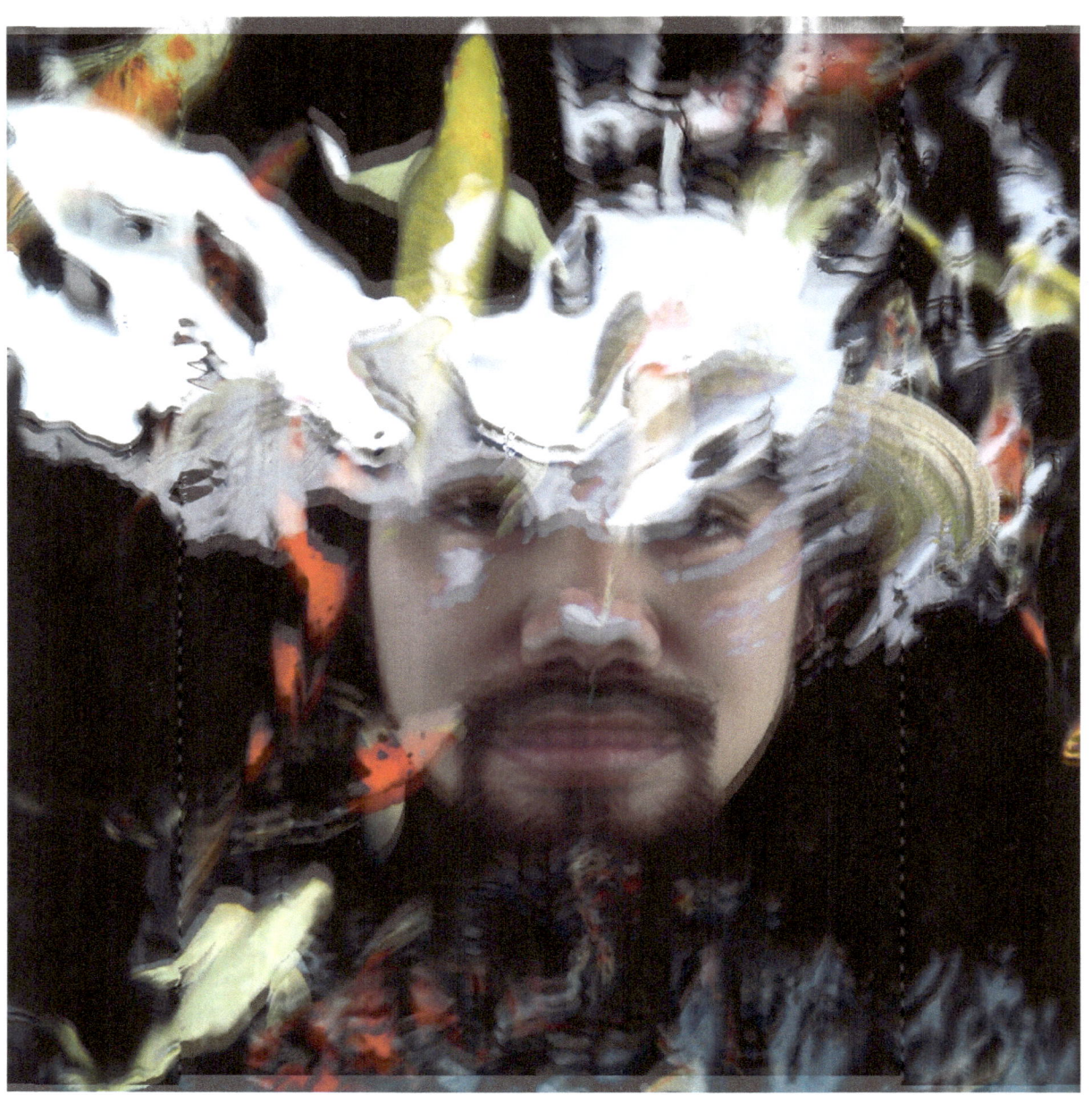

Friends are the wanting

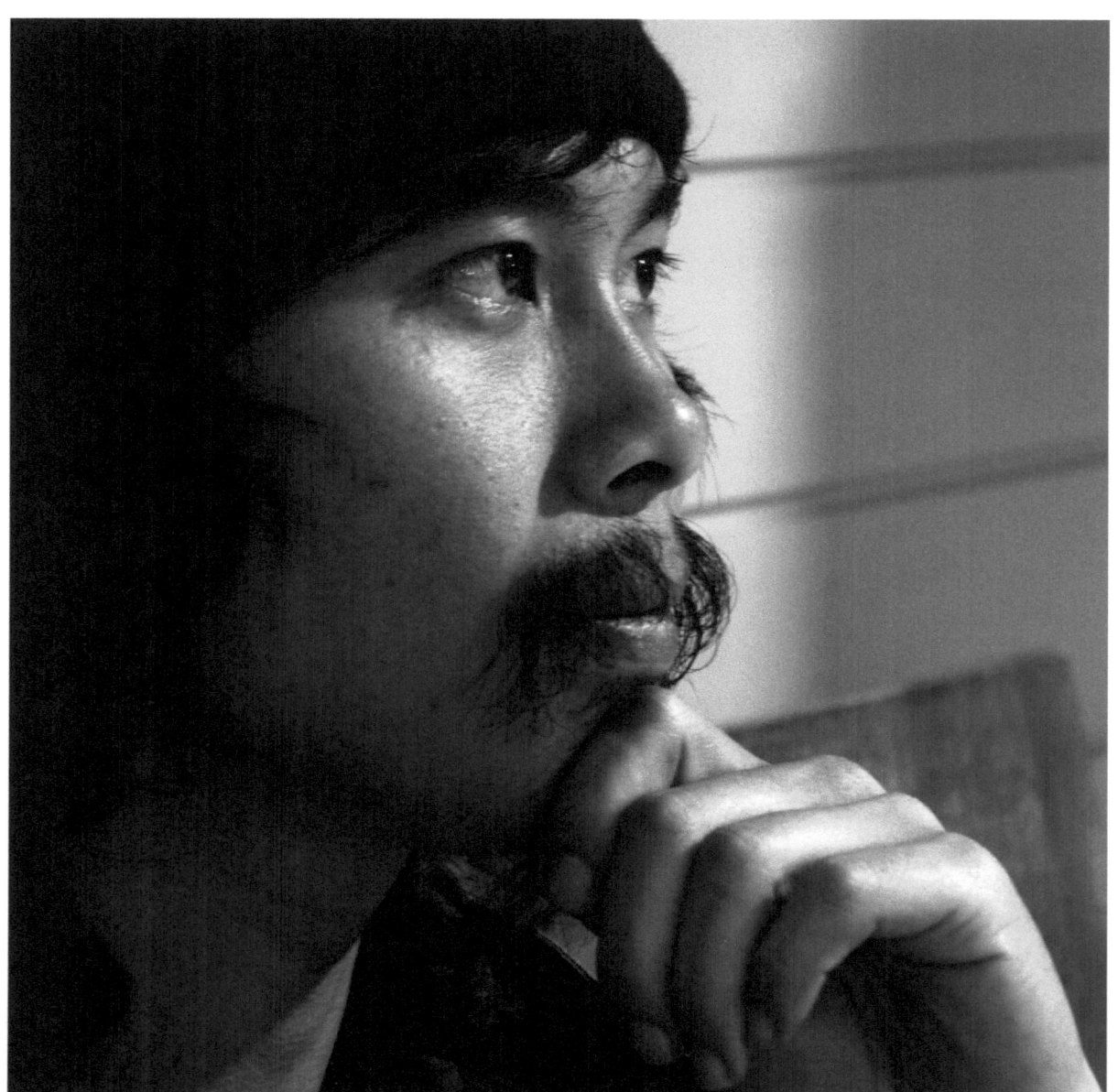

Time, the journey nowhere

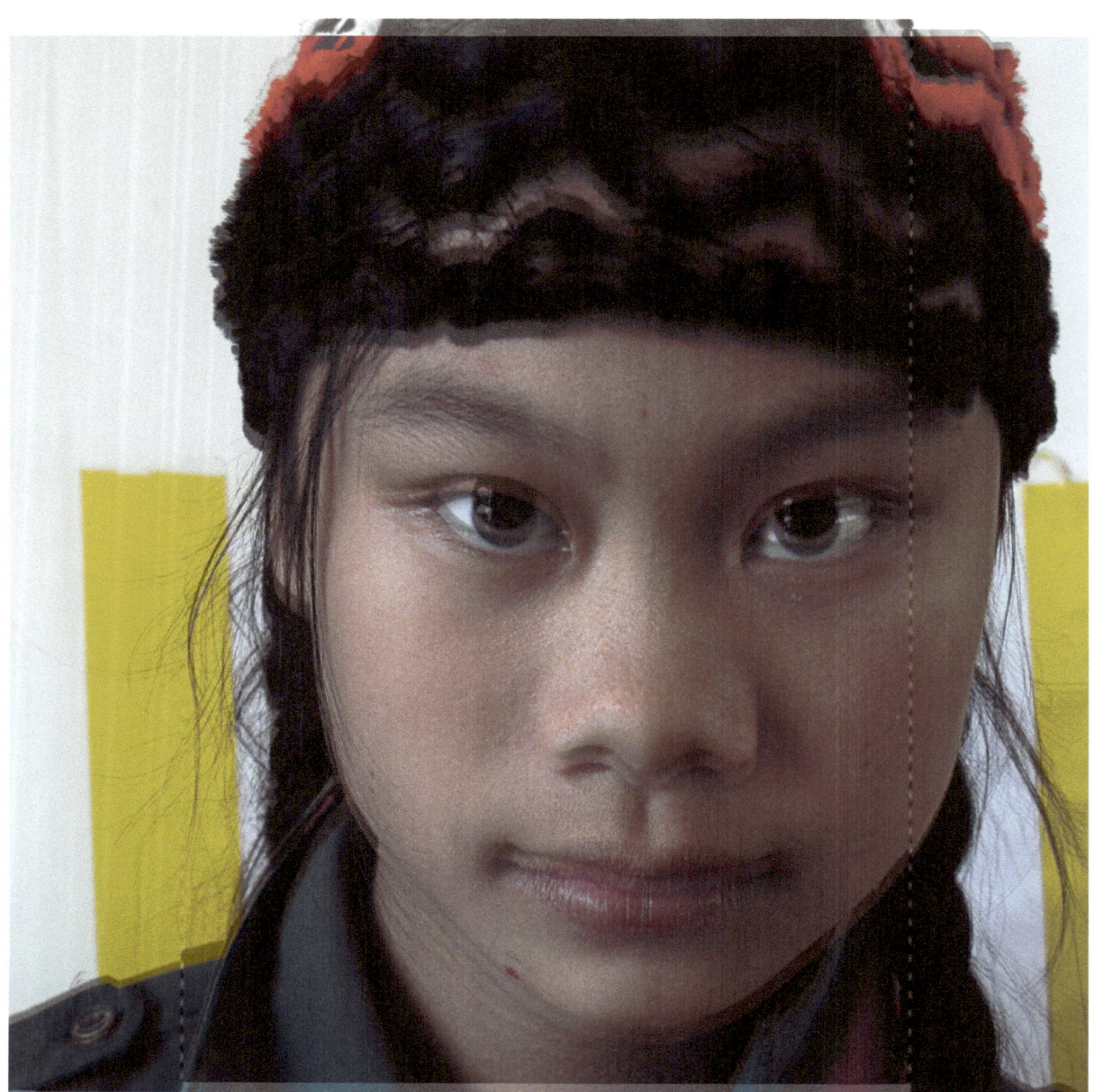

Don't fear love
it will run to you

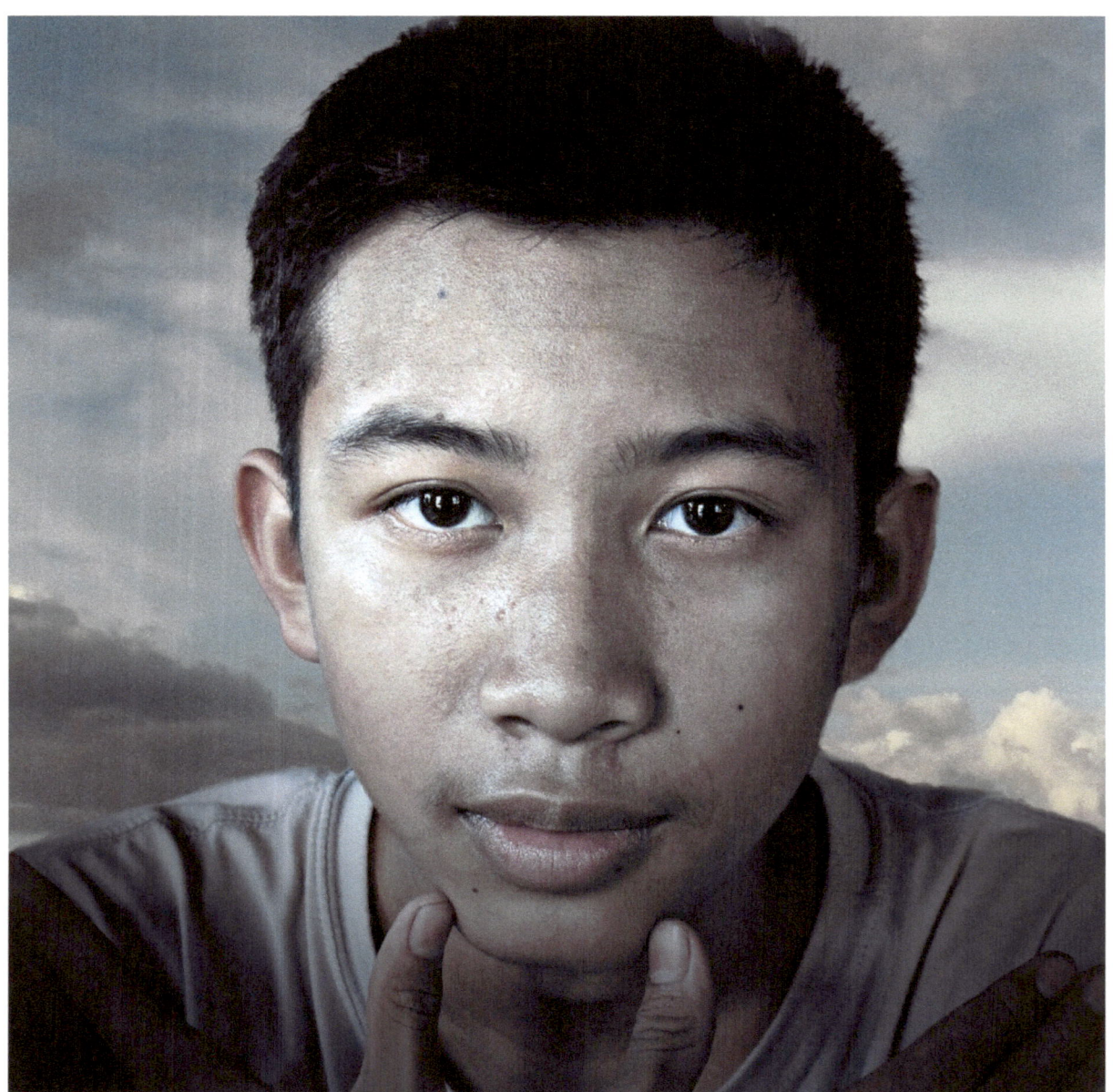

It all takes courage

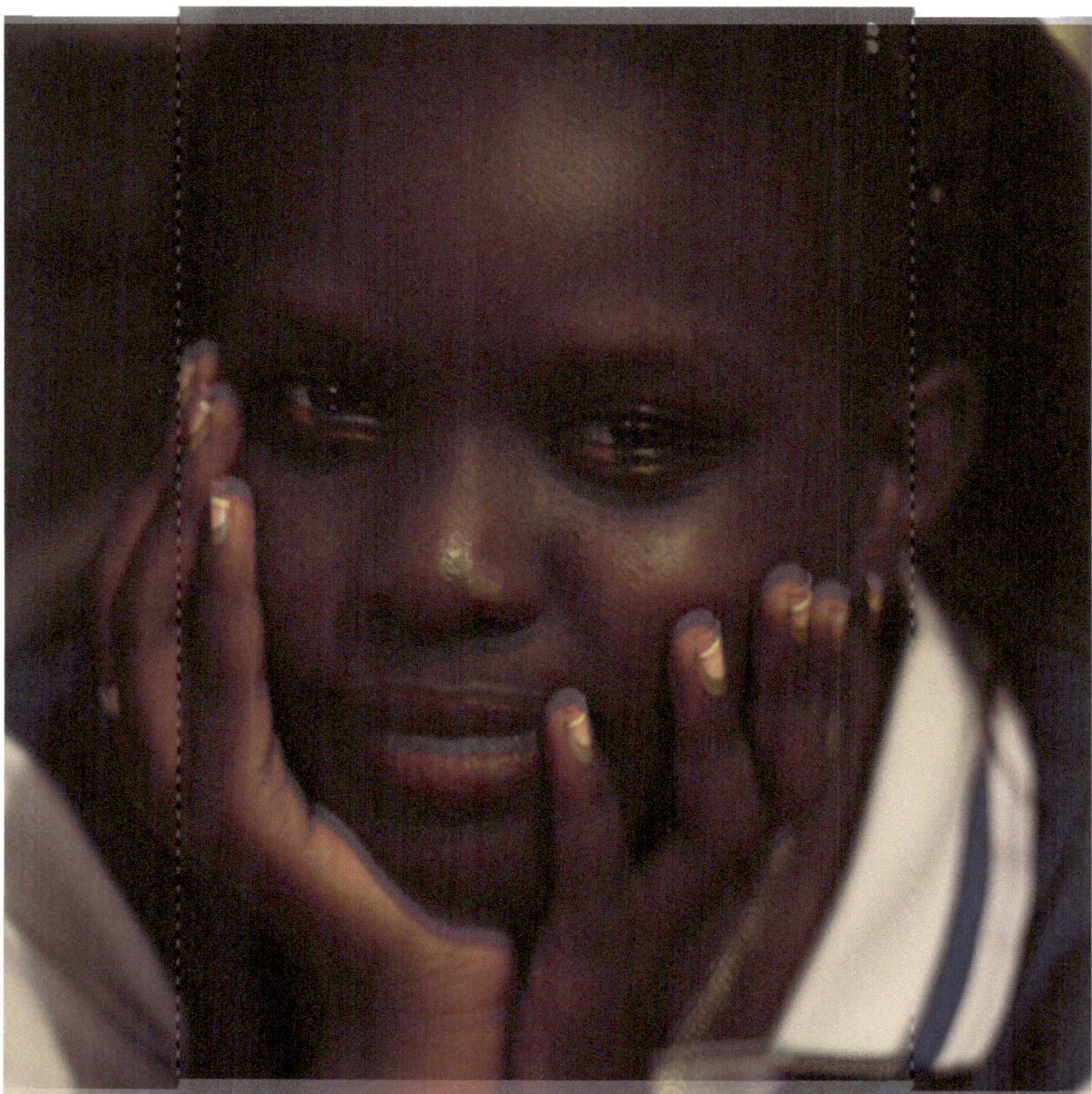

Marriage of ying and yang

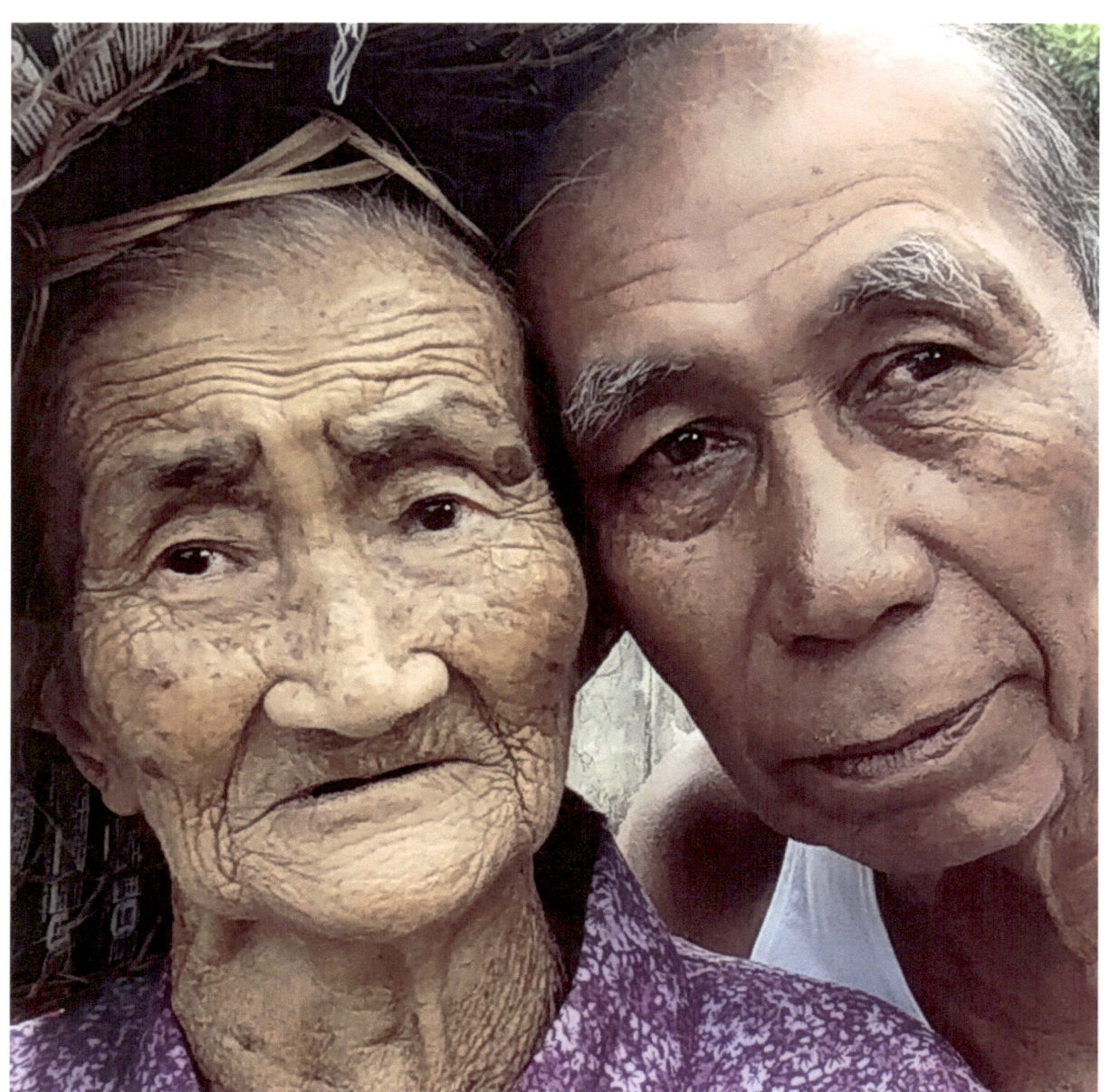

Love is an upper thing

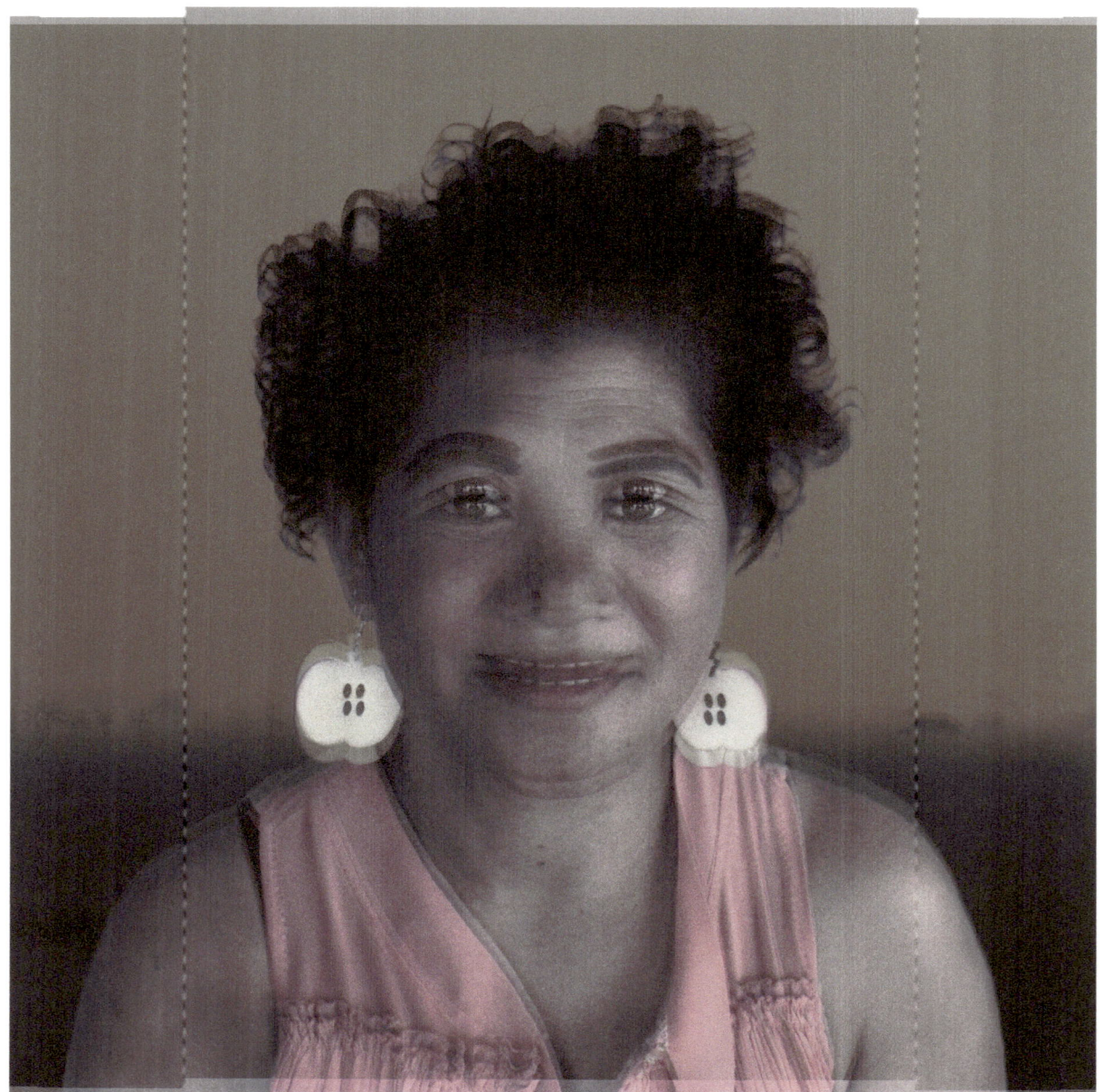

Wake up one morning

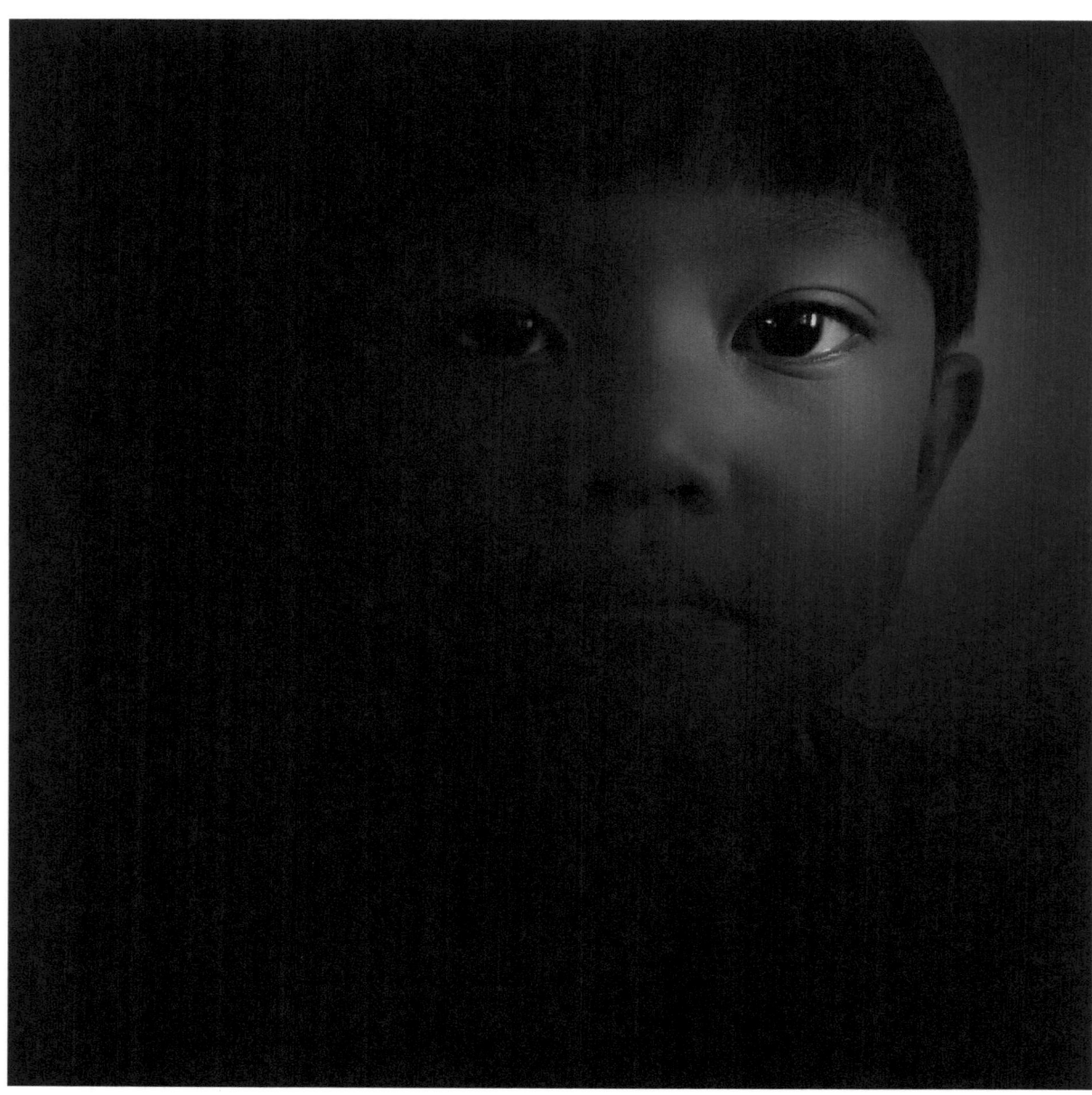

Fear of what?

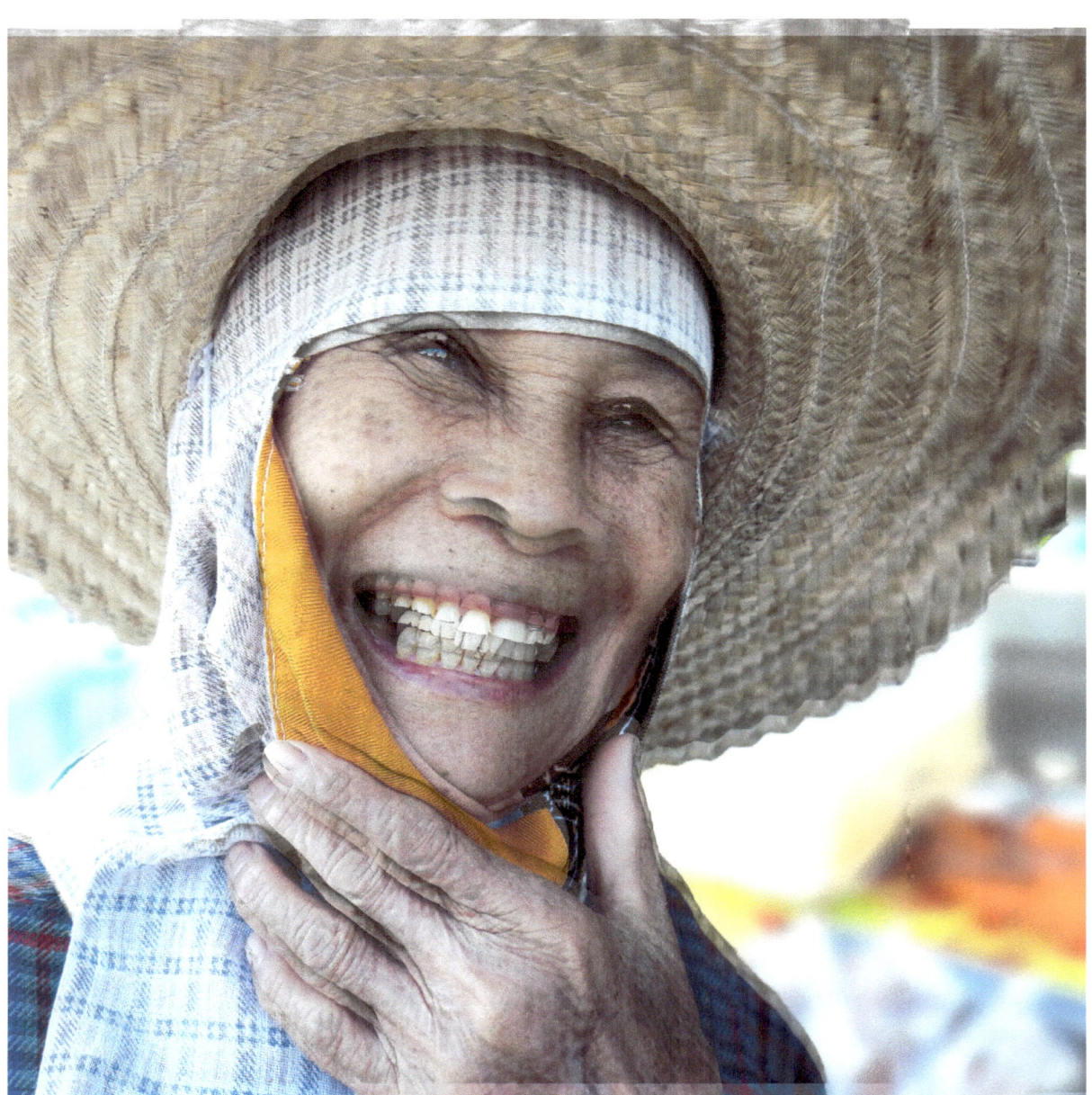

My heart is waving

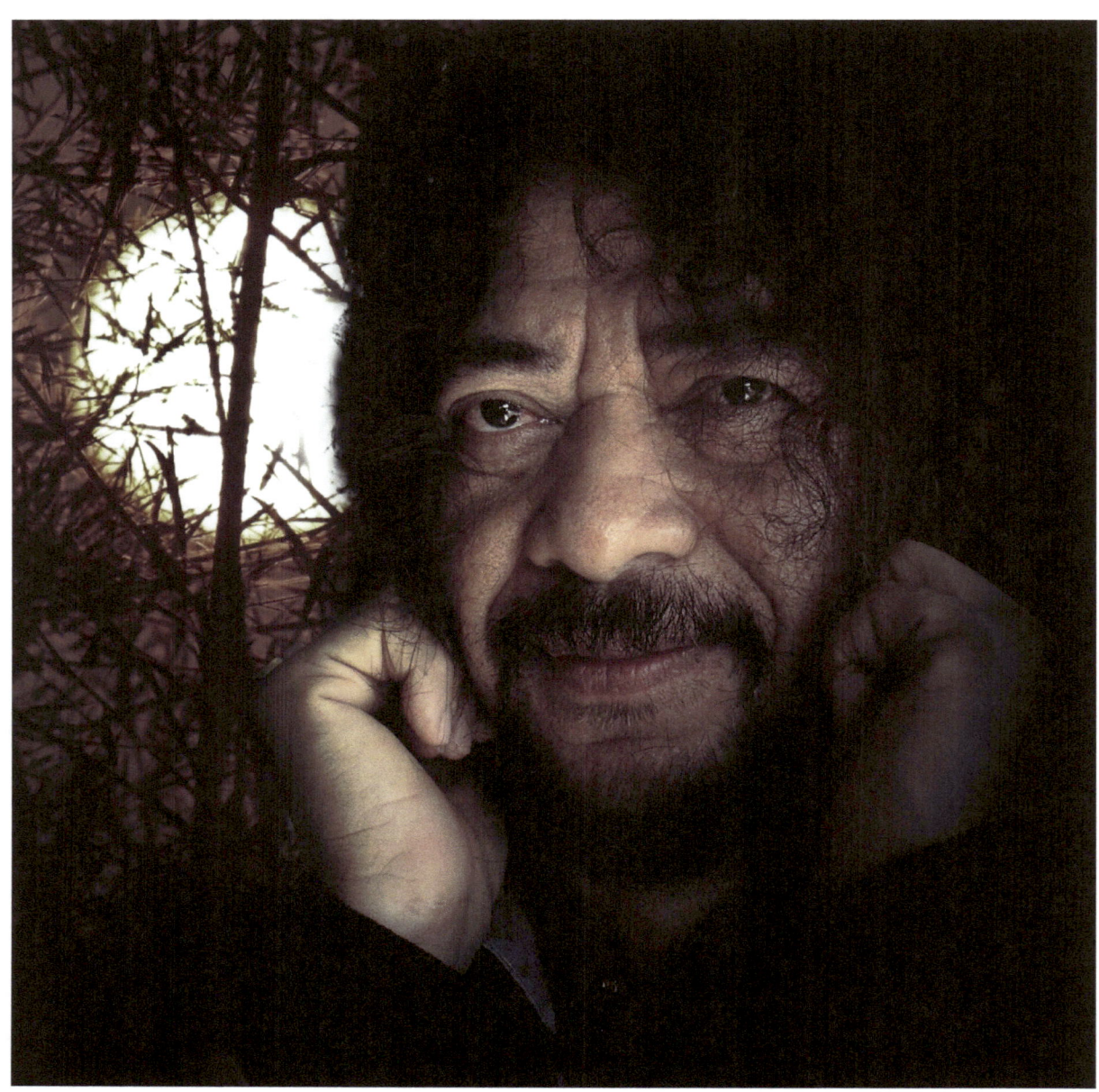

Time, the journey nowhere

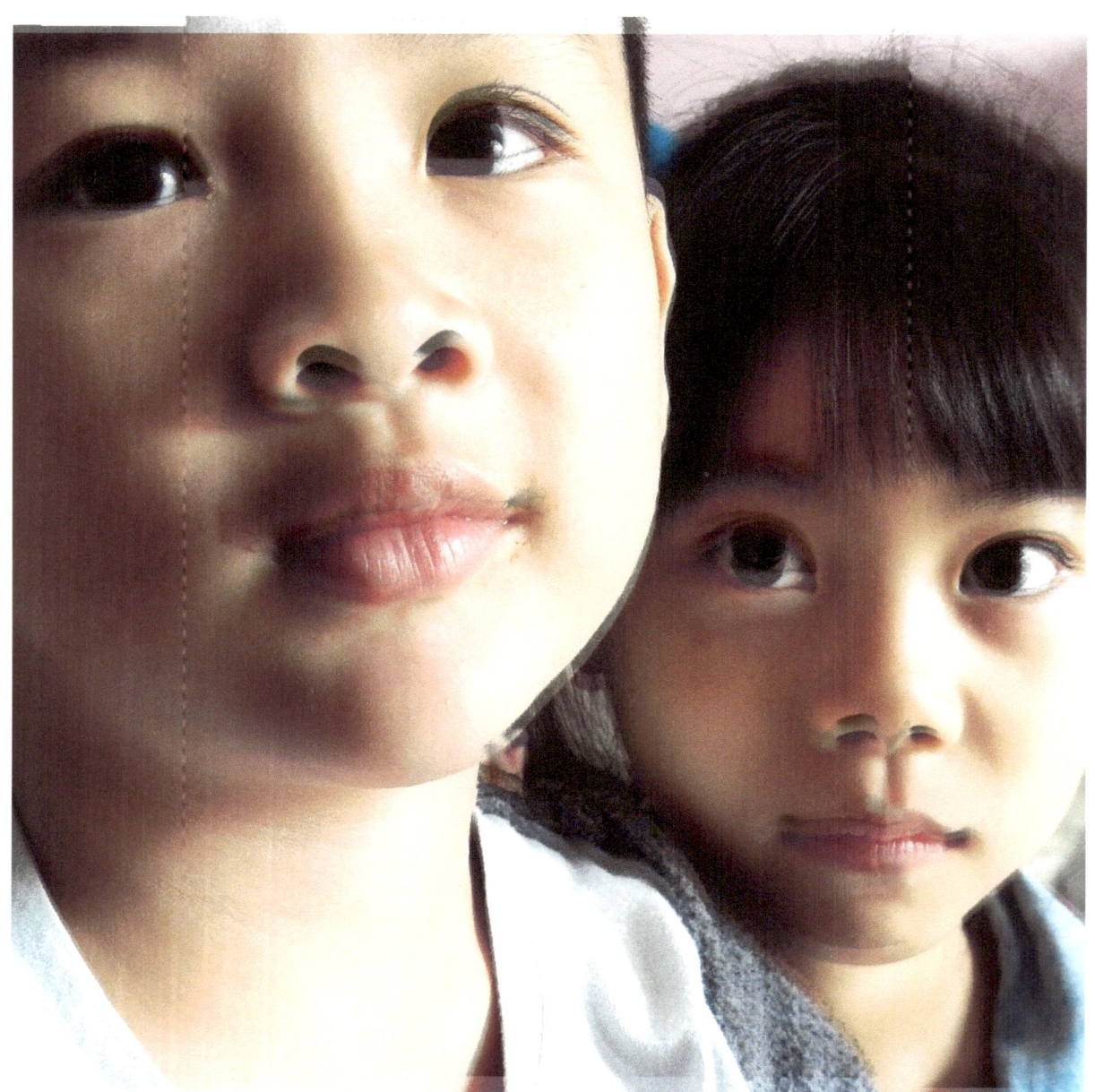

Seeking that which
is found

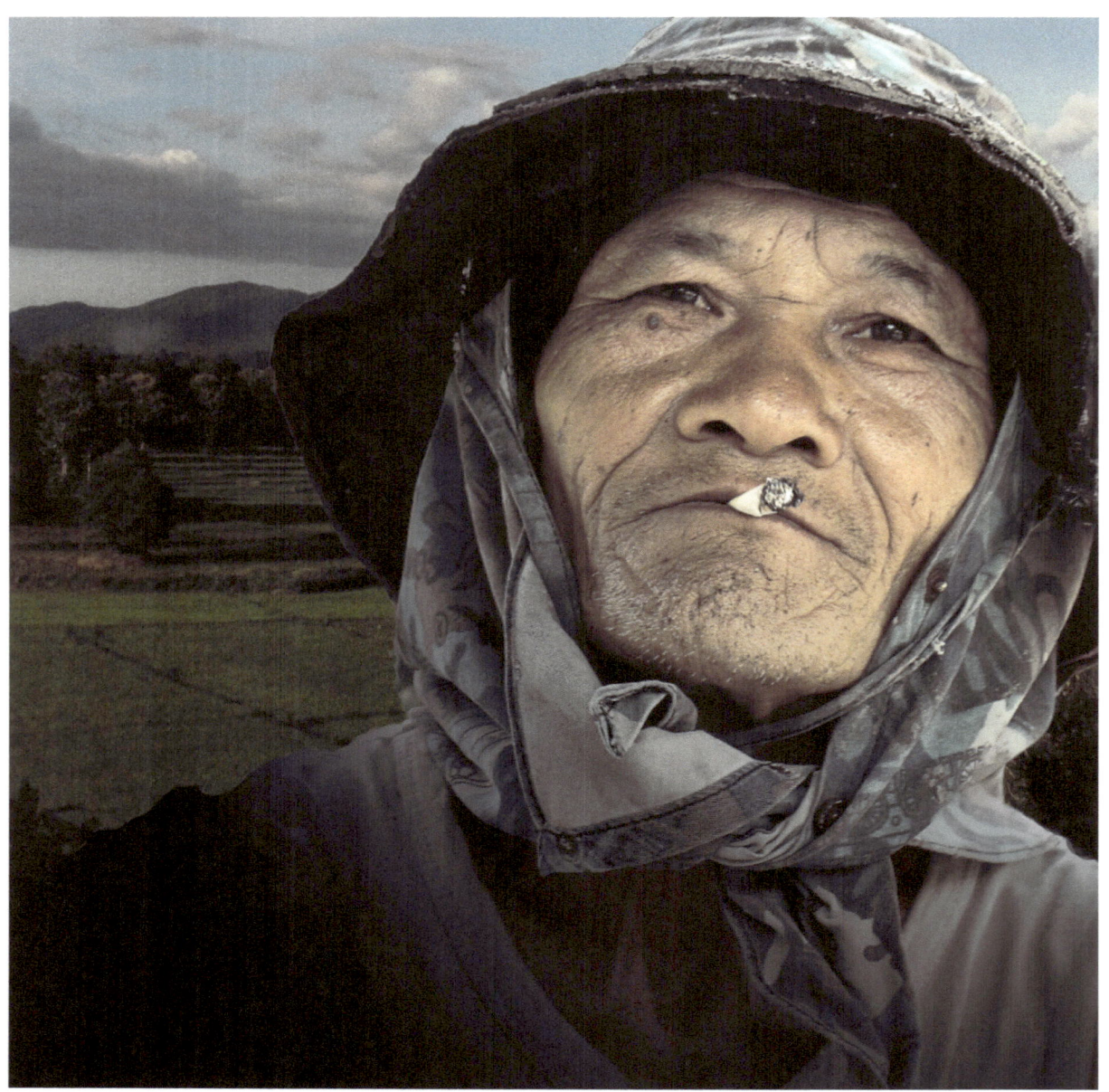

What is important to you,
is the most important

Thank you for purchasing this small book of my photos and words.

Roditch

There is a world between what we believe and what we feel and I am exploring it.

roditch@protonmail.com

www.ingramcontent.com/pod-product-compliance
Lightning Source LLC
Chambersburg PA
CBHW051953210526
45473CB00024B/2135